Keys to Receiving Your Miracle

Keys to Receiving Your Miracle

© 2016 by Bill Vincent.

All rights reserved. No part of this book may be reproduced, stored in a retrieval system or transmitted in any form or by any means without the prior written permission of the publishers, except by a reviewer who may quote brief passages in a review to be printed in a newspaper, magazine or journal.

Softcover 978-1-60796-985-3

PUBLISHED BY REVIVAL WAVES OF GLORY BOOKS & PUBLISHING

www.revivalwavesofgloryministries.com

Litchfield, IL

Published in the United States of America

Keys to Receiving Your Miracle
(Second Edition)
Miracles Happen Today

By: Bill Vincent

Keys to Receiving Your Miracle

Table of Contents

Introduction 5
Repentance Leads to Healing 6
Jesus Heals Today 25
Sovereignty 28
Receive Healing Now 43
Sickness Has to Go 46
Miracle Road Blocks 52
Miracles Happen Today 85
About The Author 108
Recommended Books 109

Introduction

I have seen the Church in a major need of Miracles. I believe the price has been paid but there are still a large amount of people afflicted.

You are about to discover that it is God's will for you to be healed and God does not put sickness upon His people. This book is going to start out with repentance and then to God's love provide health. The last two Chapters will be what every believer needs. Why don't miracles happen will release some evidence in your life, Church and even family who may deal with this much needed topic? Also what is it that makes miracles happen for some that so many don't receive? This is a smaller book packed with all you need to receive your miracle.

Repentance Leads to Healing

One of the biggest things that will cause you to lose your miracle is repentance. This vital message reveals not only why God is so willing to heal us, but why it's in His very nature to do so. As I emphasize the key role that repentance plays in releasing mercy and healing, you'll come to appreciate the beauty of repentance and how it leads to miracles. We will also examine what "Egypt" symbolizes as well as exposing several unholy attitudes that keep healing and miracles from manifesting. Be encouraged as you press into God's heart for healing! That's our God! Perhaps you've been hearing or reading about some of the wonderful healing miracles taking place over the last three years and you're saying, "I've heard some of the testimonies and I need a miracle, I need healing."

I'm sure that you are contending for healing for yourself; and you're praying for your loved ones and other people that you know. So, today, I want to encourage you. Jesus Christ is with you and He is moved with compassion to heal every kind of sickness and every kind of disease among every race, tribe or tongue! His compassion compels Him to heal! You need to believe God for a breakthrough! Allow this Chapter to minister to your heart; it's really a love letter to you, from His heart to your heart. And along with that message comes my hope and prayer for you today, that you receive a revelation of the Father's heart. When you've got this revelation, you've got a revelation of Jesus.

John 14:9 Jesus saith unto him, Have I been so long time with you, and yet hast thou not known me, Philip? he that hath seen me hath seen the Father; and how sayest thou *then,* Shew us the Father?

My prayer, too, is that you come to a full understanding of His great, big, heart of love for you! Receive this gift from His heart a revelation about repentance; then within that, His mercy; and within that, His healing. His touch for you! And repentance is the key. Now, let's go on to examine how repentance brings the breakthrough.

Repentance

When we think about repentance we think about John the Baptist.

Matthew 3:2 And saying, Repent ye: for the kingdom of heaven is at hand.

We think about fire and brimstone, and about somebody preaching hard against sin. I believe in that message, don't get me wrong! We need to have a message of holiness, separation, and consecration. There's a place, and there's a price, for that message. But as we examine repentance here, I'm talking about it in a different way than some people usually think in the context of mercy and healing.

In this context is a revelation that repentance brings mercy, and mercy brings healing. In fact, that revelation illustrates why I love to repent and get right with God! And so I want to help you get into that place of repentance where you pull the rip cord and receive both mercy and healing which is the blessing of God. About the word mercy, it is actually translated from Greek as compassion in Strong's Exhaustive Concordance: #1653 and #1656. When you see the mercy of God you see the compassion of Christ and it's always in the context of Jesus being moved with compassion, healing every sickness and disease among the people. Mercy and compassion are inseparable. But what brings you into mercy (and compassion) is repentance. So, when you see repentance, you see mercy. And what do you see when you see mercy Healing! Repentance, mercy and healing, which is why I believe that repentance is the most beautiful thing in the Bible it always brings you into a miracle.

The word repent means to turn from sin and dedicate oneself to the amendment of one's life; to change one's mind, and to bring forth fruit worthy of repentance (Webster Online Dictionary). Genuine repentance is such a radical change in the life of a person that when you look at their character afterwards, you see fruit worthy of repentance. You can tell that something has happened!

The Lord is Willing!

It isn't just the will of God to release compassion and mercy; it is the willingness of God. The Lord is willing! Yet, people so often wonder if the Lord wants to heal them.

Matthew 8:2 And, behold, there came a leper and worshipped him, saying, Lord, if thou wilt, thou canst make me clean.

For a lot of Christians, even those who believe He is willing, there is still doubt.

Their theology assures them that He is willing but still, in their heart, they react to God with "If" and "Well, God would You?" and "Oh God, could I have the grace to at least bear with it until You give it to me." We need to come to that place where we have such a solid revelation of God's heart His compassion and mercy that we see His willingness, not just His will. The thing I love most about the willingness of Jesus is in Matthew 8 (and I call that particular chapter, The Willingness of Jesus). It's the response of Jesus to the leper. He put out His hand and touched him, saying, "I am willing; be cleansed" (v. 3). Immediately his leprosy was cleansed. Next, right on the heels of that miracle was the Roman centurion, a Gentile, pleading with Jesus to heal his servant, who was lying paralyzed and tormented at home. Immediately Jesus was willing!

Matthew 8:7 And Jesus saith unto him, I will come and heal him.

Matthew 8:8, 9 The centurion answered and said, Lord, I am not worthy that thou shouldest come under my roof: but speak the word only, and my servant shall be healed. For I am a man under authority, having soldiers under me: and I say to this *man,* Go, and he goeth; and to another, Come, and he cometh; and to my servant, Do this, and he doeth *it.*

You know the rest, how Jesus commended the centurion and healed his servant at that moment. Then, as if that wasn't enough, Jesus walks into Peter's mother-in-law's house and sees her lying on the bed with a fever, walks up to her, touches her, and rebukes the fever. I mean it's just a chapter of willingness! "I am willing, be cleansed." "I will come and heal him." Walks into the house, "Awe, look she has a fever got to get rid of that!" touches her, heals her! That's my Jesus! That's your Jesus! He's the same yesterday, today, and forever!

Repentance Releases God's Nature to Bless You

Let's take a look at why it's in God's nature to be so willing to heal by taking a look at the Word of the Lord that came to the Prophet Joel:

Joel 2:12, 13 Therefore also now, saith the LORD, turn ye *even* to me with all your heart, and with fasting, and with weeping, and with mourning: And rend your heart, and not your garments, and turn unto the LORD your God: for he *is* gracious and merciful, slow to anger, and of great kindness, and repenteth him of the evil.

That verse proves that God is good. God doesn't do a good thing, God doesn't just have goodness. God is good. God is unchanging. God is eternal. God doesn't do good things. God doesn't have goodness. God is good. He can't be anything else but good. And He's eternally good. He doesn't just have goodness and do good things; He is the very substance of goodness.

God doesn't just have mercy. God is mercy. He can't be anything else but mercy. It's who He is; His eternal, unchanging nature is good, and He is mercy. He can't but be doing good things. He can't but be merciful. He is mercy and He is good.

Joel 2:13, 14 And rend your heart, and not your garments, and turn unto the LORD your God: for he *is* gracious and merciful, slow to anger, and of great kindness, and repenteth him of the evil. Who knoweth *if* he will return and repent, and leave a blessing behind him; *even* a meat offering and a drink offering unto the LORD your God?

He is of such a great kindness, that He even relents from doing harm. Who knows if He will turn and relent and leave a blessing behind Him? He is willing because He is good and He is mercy.

It's the nature of God when you repent, turn, make a change, and bring forth the fruit of repentance that He not only forgives you, but in return, He turns your captivity around by redeeming and restoring the effects of what you did in your sin. It's in the nature of God to bless. He just turns and leaves a blessing. What's so "above and beyond" is that you might not even feel that you're worthy of His blessing. You might just be thinking how getting things right and being forgiven is all you want or all there is. But because of God's love for you and by His very nature, He says, "I just don't want to forgive you, I want to forgive you because I am mercy and I'm of such great kindness, not only do I want to forgive you, but I want to leave a blessing. I want to turn around and give you that which you don't even think you're worthy to receive.

All because it's who I am. Now let Me give you a blessing." God's very nature is blessing. He is willing because He is the blessing! God is of great kindness.

You might be still be asking, "Why would God want to heal me?" You might have it down theologically; the theology part is fine. But listen. When your belief partners with faith and with the revelation of God's kindness and mercy, and you understand that when you repent He relents and leaves a blessing, then you can't help but realize why God would want to heal you! Hosea 6:1 Come, and let us return unto the LORD: for he hath torn, and he will heal us; he hath smitten, and he will bind us up.

It's like God is saying, "I want you to repent because I want to heal you." When you think about that, who wouldn't want to repent!

Romans 2:4 Or despisest thou the riches of his goodness and forbearance and longsuffering; not knowing that the goodness of God leadeth thee to repentance?

Right now, you may be sensing the Holy Spirit's touch, drawing you, bringing conviction to you that it's time to repent.

Allow the Holy Spirit to search your heart, take time with Him to deal with the things that He is pointing out to you. It will be a real key to unlock the mercy of God and His healing touch in your life. The word says not to harden your heart.

Hebrews 3:15, 16 While it is said, To day if ye will hear his voice, harden not your hearts, as in the provocation. For some, when they had heard, did provoke: howbeit not all that came out of Egypt by Moses.

God knows what it takes! Keep that truth in mind as we take another look at the Prophet Hosea's plea to the nation of Israel in Chapter Six, verse one. I'm going to explain more about how repentance brings healing and how God gets us into the right position so that we can receive His healing touch.

The Dealings of God Bring Repentance

On the one hand, their painful reality (being torn and stricken) was the result of their own willful sin.

But on the other hand, the Lord knew what it would take to turn their hearts back to Him. Affliction! Their difficulties, all their pain and suffering, would work in their favor. All because, under God's masterful hand, it would bring them to their senses so they could return to Him. That's God's mercy! If they would return, He would heal them and bind up their wounds "heal us bind us up." That's repentance, mercy and healing, in action! Now let's bring this closer to home. More often than we care to acknowledge, a lot of the time God has to really deal with us before we "get it" and repent. We looked at the connection between the mercy of God and the kindness of God. I explained that the kindness of God leads us to repentance. I want to emphasize that His kindness is also His "dealings" those precise difficulties prescribed by God to help us come to our senses and repent.

Just like the Israelites, God will use all the distressing pressure bearing down on us, whichever form it takes, for our good, if we let Him.

Then, when He is satisfied with what He sees, He will go on and do what He longs to do in our lives. "After two days He will revive us; on the third day He will raise us up, that we may live in His sight. Let us know, let us pursue the knowledge of the LORD. His going forth is established as the morning; He will come to us like the rain, like the latter and former rain to the earth" What a wonderful promise! Here's what it looks like. When Hosea spoke about the latter rain and the former rain, not only was he speaking about the blessing of God, fruitfulness, and harvest, he was also speaking into what everyone knew, which was, without rain, there will be no harvest. Without the latter rain, there's no crop, there's no reaping. Without the former rain, there's no sowing. You need the latter and the former for sowing and reaping, so there can be fruitfulness and blessing. The Bible says He will come like rain, like the latter and former rain. The rain brings life. We're talking about the blessing of the Lord, the rain of His Presence. He will come to us! Wow!

We're talking about the showers of blessing. We're talking about the goodness of God. We're talking about fruitfulness. We're talking about harvest. He says, "Come, let us return." That means return in every area where we have rebelled, hardened our hearts, and turned away from God. It means any kind of secret sin, any kind of backsliding, any way that our heart has been cold and we no longer have the passion that we once had for God. It means in any area where we have compromised our standard, the standard we know God wants us to live by, or in any way that we've turned from God. Maybe you're not backslidden all the way but you know there's even just maybe a small piece of your heart that you've hardened and you're ignoring God. There's a small piece of your heart that's in rebellion. There's a small piece of your heart that's got a little anger and bitterness to someone that you know God has asked you to forgive. There's a small piece of your heart that has compromised your commitment to Christ. And now you no longer live as you once lived for God. That's still backsliding.

By backing away from God even just a little, it means we've still fallen away from where we once were. And God is calling us back "Come, and let us return to the LORD." God is saying (paraphrase): "I want you to return, I want you to repent because I want to bring blessing; I want to leave a blessing behind, My manifold goodness and kindness. I want you to return to Me so that I can bind you up and heal you. If you will return then I can begin to come with the rain of My Presence again. As I begin to turn your captivity around, I want to bring you blessing and fruitfulness. I want you to repent because if you repent, I can give you mercy. And when I can give you mercy, I can give you healing. That is My heart."

Ungodly Attitudes dry up the Rain of GOD'S PRESENCE

So who wouldn't want to return to the Lord? What is it that influences people one way or the other?

Let's examine what happened to King Hezekiah, the consequences of an alliance he made with Egypt, and how the Prophet Isaiah was God's messenger to turn him back to God. I want you to see how repentance not only brought forth a miracle in his life; it affected the whole nation of Israel. Isaiah 38:1-3 In those days was Hezekiah sick unto death. And Isaiah the prophet the son of Amoz came unto him, and said unto him, Thus saith the LORD, Set thine house in order: for thou shalt die, and not live. Then Hezekiah turned his face toward the wall, and prayed unto the LORD, And said, Remember now, O LORD, I beseech thee, how I have walked before thee in truth and with a perfect heart, and have done *that which is* good in thy sight. And Hezekiah wept sore.

Something rose up in Hezekiah. Even though he was told to set his house in order because he would die, he humbled himself and contended with God! It's like he said, "I know that as I weep and repent and turn to the Lord like this, God will turn His face to me because He is merciful.

I'm going to humble myself and God is going to cause me to hear from heaven. He's going to turn and heal me and He's going to heal the land!" He could have said, "The word of the Lord has warned me to set my house in order because I'm going to die. Since God said it, I'm going to believe it. That settles it." But his attitude was: "No. I'm going to repent. I'm going to turn to the Lord. I'm going to cry out to the Lord. I'm going to weep. For some of you, the doctors have come and said your medical condition is hopeless. Maybe a negative report has come that you're going blind, or that you're losing your sight, or there's an incurable disease in your body. Or maybe there is bondage and a torment because the devil has told you you'll never be free, and so there's hopelessness and despair on you. Some of you believe that report of the doctor. Some of you believe the accusation of the accuser of the brethren. Some of you have come into the hopelessness and the despair of discouragement and you're no longer able to believe the promise of God.

My best advice is DON'T GIVE IN!

And the key is repentance. When Hezekiah repented God's mercy came upon him. But what was it that Hezekiah needed to repent of? I asked the Holy Spirit why he was sick and if there was any sin in his life. What was the door that opened him up to a terminal disease?

2 Kings 18:21-24 Now, behold, thou trustest upon the staff of this bruised reed, *even* upon Egypt, on which if a man lean, it will go into his hand, and pierce it: so *is* Pharaoh king of Egypt unto all that trust on him. But if ye say unto me, We trust in the LORD our God: *is* not that he, whose high places and whose altars Hezekiah hath taken away, and hath said to Judah and Jerusalem, Ye shall worship before this altar in Jerusalem? Now therefore, I pray thee, give pledges to my lord the king of Assyria, and I will deliver thee two thousand horses, if thou be able on thy part to set riders upon them. How then wilt thou turn away the face of one captain of the least of my master's servants,

and put thy trust on Egypt for chariots and for horsemen?

But how does this apply to us?

How have we made an alliance with Egypt? We do so when we trust in our own way, in our own strength, and in our own plan. For example, sometimes we trust more in the medical system and what the doctor says than what God says. "I'm going to trust in the arm of flesh. I'm going to trust in the arm of man. I'm going to trust in the fact that if God doesn't heal me in that crusade, I can always go to the doctor." Now don't get me wrong, I value our doctors and medical science. But I believe that if we would turn away from the alliance that some of us have made with Egypt, we will see a greater release of miracles and healing. That means where we need to repent, let's do it! After Hezekiah turned to the Lord and cried out to him in repentance God told Isaiah to tell him that He wasn't only going to give him fifteen more years to live, He was going to deliver him and his city from the king of Assyria.

God would confirm it by giving Hezekiah a great sign. He would move the sun back by ten degrees.

Keys to Receiving Your Miracle

What a great deliverance and God wants to bring a great deliverance in your life too! There comes a time when we need to allow the Lord to deal with us. By not doing so, sickness lingers and miracle healing won't happen. So let's allow the Holy Spirit to examine our hearts. Maybe there is a bitter root judgment against someone, perhaps a pastor or a leader, and words have been spoken against them. Maybe there is rebellion, jealousy and envy. Ungodly attitudes dry up the rain of God's presence. Our focus shouldn't just be about needing a physical healing miracle and concentrating on that fact. A lot of the time it's more about needing to be cleansed of "spiritual leprosy" because that is the connection and open door to our illness. I believe today God wants us to return to Him. Before mercy and healing, I believe God is saying "I want repentance." Maybe the Spirit of God has touched the attitude of your heart. Maybe you've seen something in your spirit, something that's been there and God wants to just cleanse the core of your heart.

Is there a cry for holiness and truth in your life? Do you sense God calling you to a deeper season of consecration? He wants to consecrate you. He wants His Presence to consecrate you.

Isaiah 4:4 When the Lord shall have washed away the filth of the daughters of Zion, and shall have purged the blood of Jerusalem from the midst thereof by the spirit of judgment, and by the spirit of burning.

Is there a cry in your heart for the spirit of judgment and burning to come to your life?

1 Corinthians 11:29, 30 For he that eateth and drinketh unworthily, eateth and drinketh damnation to himself, not discerning the Lord's body. For this cause many *are* weak and sickly among you, and many sleep.

Such examination isn't a place of condemnation.

Psalms 26:2 Examine me, O LORD, and prove me; try my reins and my heart.

Jesus Heals Today

Jesus is alive and still heals today. He is alive. This is a simple title that needs to be preached in every local Church. Most Christians say yes I agree that Jesus still heals but we don't see much. We need breakthrough and some of that breaking though comes from basic information.

Physical Healing

Isaiah 53:5 But he *was* wounded for our transgressions, *he was* bruised for our iniquities: the chastisement of our peace *was* upon him; and with his stripes we are healed.

1 Peter 2:24 Who his own self bare our sins in his own body on the tree, that we, being dead to sins, should live unto righteousness: by whose stripes ye were healed.

Keys to Receiving Your Miracle

3 John 1:2 Beloved, I wish above all things that thou mayest prosper and be in health, even as thy soul prospereth.

Exodus 15:26 And said, If thou wilt diligently hearken to the voice of the LORD thy God, and wilt do that which is right in his sight, and wilt give ear to his commandments, and keep all his statutes, I will put none of these diseases upon thee, which I have brought upon the Egyptians: for I *am* the LORD that healeth thee.

Matthew 9:28, 29 And when he was come into the house, the blind men came to him: and Jesus saith unto them, Believe ye that I am able to do this? They said unto him, Yea, Lord. Then touched he their eyes, saying, According to your faith be it unto you.

If Jesus was right here right now and he laid hands on you would you be healed? (YES)

The anointing breaks the yoke.

John 14:12-15 Verily, verily, I say unto you, He that believeth on me, the works that I do shall he do also; and greater *works* than these shall he do; because I go unto my Father. And whatsoever ye shall ask in my name, that will I do, that the Father may be glorified in the Son. If ye shall ask any thing in my name, I will do *it*. If ye love me, keep my commandments.

Old things are passed away all things become new. Healed Heart

Psalms 147:2, 3 The LORD doth build up Jerusalem: he gathereth together the outcasts of Israel. He healeth the broken in heart, and bindeth up their wounds.

Luke 4:18 The Spirit of the Lord *is* upon me, because he hath anointed me to preach the gospel to the poor; he hath sent me to heal the brokenhearted, to preach deliverance to the captives, and recovering of sight to the blind, to set at liberty them that are bruised, you need to believe God. You need to believe that you are going to receive.

Realize that it is God's will that you are healed.

"Jesus is the same yesterday, today, and forever."

Sovereignty

God is good. God heals because He is sovereign. This question on occasion arises in the church: "Since God is sovereign and since we don't presently see everyone healed, are we therefore correct in assuming that God sometimes does not want to heal a certain individual?" This is an honest question and therefore, with the help of the Holy Spirit, I want to begin answering it by examining God's sovereignty. Then I'll expose some of the misconceptions associated with His supremacy.

What is God's Sovereignty?

Let's take a look at the words sovereign and sovereignty as defined in the American Dictionary of the English Language.

First of all, sovereign means: supreme in power; possessing supreme dominion; as a sovereign prince. God is the sovereign ruler of the universe. Secondly, sovereignty means: supreme power; supremacy; the possession of the highest power, or of uncontrollable power. Absolute sovereignty belongs to God.

There are numerous references in the Bible to God's sovereignty, but for the sake of being brief, we'll begin this Chapter by taking a look at two scriptures. Let's go first to the Old Testament and look at a declaration about God's sovereignty that was composed by David in Psalms.

Psalms 103:18 To such as keep his covenant, and to those that remember his commandments to do them.

1 Timothy 6:15, 16 Which in his times he shall shew, *who is* the blessed and only Potentate, the King of kings, and Lord of lords; Who only hath immortality, dwelling in the light which no man can approach unto; whom no man hath seen, nor can see: to whom *be* honour and power everlasting. Amen.

God is the sovereign ruler of the universe. Total sovereignty belongs to God alone; He rules over all. The whole Bible testifies to this fact.

Now having said that, most Christians do have a measure of understanding about God's sovereignty (that He rules over all), but they often misunderstand the intentions of God's heart in the midst of His sovereignty. I say this because quite often I've noticed that when someone isn't healed (after being prayed for), some Christians will make a statement like this: "Well, God is sovereign!" What they are implying is that God wants to heal some and not others.

I'm convinced that one of the most precious truths of the Bible, and one of the most abused truths of the Bible, is about God's sovereignty. Further, I believe that God's sovereignty has been blamed for more of the devil's work than most of us realize.

Sometimes people will try to blame human failure on God's sovereignty. God Always Keeps His Word

The Bible tells us what redemption should look like, what deliverance should look like, and what healing should look like but so often we fail to appropriate these truths. Sometimes this happens because of the opposition of the enemy.

Ephesians 6:10, 11 Finally, my brethren, be strong in the Lord, and in the power of his might. Put on the whole armour of God, that ye may be able to stand against the wiles of the devil.

1 Peter 5:8 Be sober, be vigilant; because your adversary the devil, as a roaring lion, walketh about, seeking whom he may devour:

Our response is often like this when we see that someone isn't healed: "I know God promises healing and I know He says in His word that He will heal all our diseases.

Psalms 103:3 Who forgiveth all thine iniquities; who healeth all thy diseases;

Some will say; but God is sovereign and sometimes He will go against even what He promised in His word." What an absurd statement! That kind of attitude is an insult to God's character, disguised as religious humility.

The fact is God always upholds His word! In the middle of experiencing God's faithfulness, kindness and favor, David wrote:

Psalms 138:2 I will worship toward thy holy temple, and praise thy name for thy lovingkindness and for thy truth: for thou hast magnified thy word above all thy name.

He knew first hand that God keeps His word. You know, God is compelled to keep His word, and not because He is obligated, but because He wants to. We can trust in His faithfulness at all times.

Numbers 23:19 God *is* not a man, that he should lie; neither the son of man, that he should repent: hath he said, and shall he not do *it?* or hath he spoken, and shall he not make it good?

In God, we can truly trust His Word. We have an enemy, the devil, who wants to lure us from trusting God by distorting the truth about His character. Jesus called the devil a thief. Look at what Jesus said about the devil and then see what He said about Himself:

John 10:10 The thief cometh not, but for to steal, and to kill, and to destroy: I am come that they might have life, and that they might have *it* more abundantly.

Jesus wants us to have life and to have it more abundantly. He is always speaking life into our circumstances. We need to lean into that truth. And I'm sure such a life giving revelation would put a stop to most of the spiritual abuse that happens from time to time. I say that because I've seen some people in ministry acting in a very cruel manner when someone isn't healed by saying that if they didn't get healed, then it's their own fault. They assume their healing is not manifesting because of reasons like these: unbelief; not enough faith; not doing enough; hidden sin in the person's life; or demonic bondage.

Yes, there might be unbelief, or hidden sin etc., but it's not helping when people point the finger and make assumptions and "hang that over someone's head." That's called abuse. And when someone is afflicted by spiritual abuse, the devil will always try to exploit the situation further in order to stop the person from pursuing and gaining a complete healing. This must not be allowed to happen! So I just want to speak a word of encouragement to those of you who may have been on the receiving end of some kind of spiritual abuse. Please take counsel with a mature believer that you trust (or a chosen few mature believers) so that you can come to a place of forgiveness and healing for this wounding and then proceed with receiving your full healing. Keep pressing in.

God Rules in History

The Scriptures teach that God is the unlimited, sovereign, reigning Lord, who has reconciled the world to Himself, through His Son Jesus Christ, the Messiah.

Roman 5:8-11 But God commendeth his love toward us, in that, while we were yet sinners, Christ died for us. Much more then, being now justified by his blood, we shall be saved from wrath through him. For if, when we were enemies, we were reconciled to God by the death of his Son, much more, being reconciled, we shall be saved by his life. And not only *so,* but we also joy in God through our Lord Jesus Christ, by whom we have now received the atonement.

God does not manipulate or force His creation. The foundations of His throne are righteousness and justice.

Psalms 89:14 Justice and judgment *are* the habitation of thy throne: mercy and truth shall go before thy face.

One day every knee will bow and every tongue will confess that Jesus Christ is Lord.

Philippians 2:10, 11 That at the name of Jesus every knee should bow, of *things* in heaven, and *things* in earth, and *things* under the earth; And *that* every tongue should confess that Jesus Christ *is* Lord, to the glory of God the Father.

God's people are under His delegated authority. What a safe place!

God is sovereign and it is scripturally true and evident. You know, everything is going to end up exactly where He says it will. But we sometimes mistakenly assume that God overrides or bypasses human initiative and that He alone, by Himself, wants to have the devil completely under His control. Now the devil is completely controlled by God, but God wants us to take our position of delegated authority, responsibly, against the devil's schemes. God wants to involve us in opposing the kingdom of darkness as well as advancing His kingdom.

Here's a thought. If God's perfect sovereign will is being completely worked out in time, in space, and in history apart from human effort and involvement, then why in the world have a kingdom of God where Christ's authority is manifested?

In fact, if God is sovereign in the unscriptural way some believers say He is, then why have Jesus come? The church's misunderstanding about God's sovereignty promotes a mindset that thinks it's God's will that people aren't healed. With that kind of attitude then they say, for instance, that God in His sovereignty wants a person to stay deaf. Let's think about that, because if a deaf person is convinced that is true, then using a hearing aid would be against God's will. If, as some in the church think, "God's sovereignty" means He is controlling everything and all is going just the way He wants it to, then why change anything? The exact opposite is true!

Jesus came and absolutely devastated all evil and He came representing completely and perfectly, the will of His Father.

John 5:17-32 But Jesus answered them, My Father worketh hitherto, and I work. Therefore the Jews sought the more to kill him, because he not only had broken the sabbath, but said also that God was his Father, making himself equal with God. Then answered Jesus and said unto them, Verily, verily, I say unto you, The Son can do nothing of himself, but what he seeth the Father do: for what things soever he doeth, these also doeth the Son likewise. For the Father loveth the Son, and sheweth him all things that himself doeth: and he will shew him greater works than these, that ye may marvel. For as the Father raiseth up the dead, and quickeneth *them;* even so the Son quickeneth whom he will. For the Father judgeth no man, but hath committed all judgment unto the Son: That all *men* should honour the Son, even as they honour the Father. He that honoureth not the Son honoureth not the Father which hath sent him. Verily, verily, I say unto you, He that heareth my word, and believeth on him that sent me, hath everlasting life, and shall not come into condemnation; but is passed from death unto life. Verily, verily, I say unto you, The hour is coming, and now is, when the dead shall hear the voice of the Son of God: and they that hear shall live. For as the Father hath life in himself; so hath he given to the Son to have life in himself; And hath given him authority to execute judgment also, because he is the Son of man. Marvel not at this: for the hour is coming, in the which all that are in the graves shall hear his voice, And shall come forth; they that have done good, unto the resurrection of life; and they that have done evil, unto the resurrection of damnation. I can of mine own self do nothing: as I hear, I judge: and my judgment is just; because I seek not mine own will, but the will of the Father which hath sent me. If I bear witness of myself, my witness is not true. There is another that beareth witness of me; and I know that the witness which he witnesseth of me is true.

Here's what Jesus would say: "I represent God's total lordship and rule. When you look at Me you see God's rule in operation, you see God's heart. Are you sick? Be healed! Are you demonized? Be delivered! Are you hungry? Be fed! Are you naked? Be clothed! Are you poor? Receive of My abundance!" Then He says, "Now, go in my name and do the same!"

In other words, represent Jesus accurately, and show people what the Father is really like. Why? So people can truly know the Father and His character.

God Wants Co-laborers

However, we have teaching that says the devil (who causes sickness, disease and premature death) can't commit deeds of darkness unless God sovereignly wills it. But such teaching makes it seem like when people are sick or they die, that it must be God's will because He is sovereign. I disagree! Where does that kind of teaching leave us? It leaves us without the ministry of Jesus.

Hebrews 1:2 Hath in these last days spoken unto us by *his* Son, whom he hath appointed heir of all things, by whom also he made the worlds;

God has spoken to us in His Son whom He appointed heir of all things. God's will is fully disclosed in Jesus; in His actions and by His words. His actions and words disclose that His Father is the supreme ruler. However, there are pockets of "rebel territory" on planet earth where God's will is not carried out or not carried out fully. Further, we see that sickness and disease interrupt and impair the outworking of the will of God.

An accepting type of sovereignty thinking, which is more pagan than scriptural, robs the church of both its mandate and its authority! Then believers are blinded and they're not crying out like this: "Where are the miracles of our forefathers?" Instead they are saying, "Don't you know God is sovereign? Don't you know He's got the devil on a leash?" Look. We have been robbed. We need to know that yes, God is sovereign, but He wants us take our rightful place and co-labor with Him to contest and defeat the devil's schemes. Our mandate is to advance the kingdom of God under the authority of God.

To be well equipped for defeating the enemy, we need to know the enemy's "mode of operation."

Peter (the apostle) wrote to his fellow believers:
1 Peter 5:8 Be sober, be vigilant; because your adversary the devil, as a roaring lion, walketh about, seeking whom he may devour:

Ezekiel said that God looked for a man who would make a wall, and stand in the gap before Him on behalf of the land (because of wickedness), that He should not destroy it, but He found no one.

Ezekiel 22:30 And I sought for a man among them, that should make up the hedge, and stand in the gap before me for the land, that I should not destroy it: but I found none.

As well, Isaiah said that God was displeased because truth and justice were lacking and there was no one to intercede. So His own arm brought salvation for Him and His own righteousness sustained Him.

Isaiah 59:16, 17 And he saw that *there was* no man, and wondered that *there was* no intercessor: therefore his arm brought salvation unto him; and his righteousness, it sustained him. For he put on righteousness as a breastplate, and an helmet of salvation upon his head; and he put on the garments of vengeance *for* clothing, and was clad with zeal as a cloke.

The message of both Ezekiel and Isaiah are so significant! Each one points to the fact that God is seeking at least one person to co-labor with Him so that the enemy's plans are overthrown and God's plans are birthed in the earth. God is sovereign, but He wants us to call upon Him to execute His mercy. Intercession is calling on God to be merciful.

God Acts in Perfect Justice

Remember, righteousness and justice is the foundation of God's throne. In fact, they are like pillars fortifying His sovereignty!

With this in mind, based on the facts presented about God's sovereignty, I believe that the "honest question" posed at the beginning of this teaching must be answered like this. Even though we don't see everyone healed, it's incorrect to assume that God sometimes doesn't want to heal a certain individual. Because of His mercy and sovereignty I am convinced that He does not discriminate against anyone who comes to Him for healing.

Today, you may be standing in faith, pressing in for healing. Or maybe you are nearly overcome with unbelief and saying to yourself, "O, forget it!" Please don't give up! We're praying for your breakthrough whether you're standing in faith or you're fighting off unbelief. Also, I'd like to help you further by recommending an excellent Book: Defeating the Demonic Realm. It will help break roots, spirits and curses for sicknesses.

Receive Healing Now

The price has already been paid for. So today is a great day to be healed. The Bible declares in Heb 13:8, "Jesus Christ is the same yesterday, today and forever."

If He healed all the sick 2000 years ago then He stills heals all the sick today.

Matthew 8:16 When the even was come, they brought unto him many that were possessed with devils: and he cast out the spirits with *his* word, and healed all that were sick:

Does He want to heal you?

Matthew 8:2, 3 And, behold, there came a leper and worshipped him, saying, Lord, if thou wilt, thou canst make me clean. And Jesus put forth *his* hand, and touched him, saying, I will; be thou clean. And immediately his leprosy was cleansed.

Jesus is willing!

God is a God of love and shows no partiality. I am willing, Be Healed!

Isaiah 53:4, 5 Surely he hath borne our griefs, and carried our sorrows: yet we did esteem him stricken, smitten of God, and afflicted. But he *was* wounded for our transgressions, *he was* bruised for our iniquities: the chastisement of our peace *was* upon him; and with his stripes we are healed.

You can see that the cross was to set you free from sin and sickness. When He said on the cross, "It is finished" He declared freedom from sin, sickness and death. Be healed in Jesus name.

Romans 8:11 But if the Spirit of him that raised up Jesus from the dead dwell in you, he that raised up Christ from the dead shall also quicken your mortal bodies by his Spirit that dwelleth in you.

Meditate on this reality, "The same Spirit that raised Jesus from the dead dwells in

Keys to Receiving Your Miracle

YOU!" Let resurrection power be released! You can be healed now! Put your hand on your sickness and say, "Thank you Jesus for healing me, I cancel this sickness and declare I am free, I receive my miracle right now Father, In Jesus Name, Amen

Sickness Has to Go

There is a freedom we all can receive from sickness. I think that when Jesus told the disciples to preach the gospel and heal the sick, He meant whatever city or town they entered to heal the sick there. Whatever city or town they went to, He was saying to heal the sick in that place.

I have a hard time believing that God would give anyone a disease. It is not God's will that a person be paralyzed. I am talking about covenant children. I know about the principle of sin and how that if we open a door for sin and disease, it can be allowed in by God. I am talking about mercy triumphing over judgment when we are in right relationship with God.

SUFFERING FOR JESUS

James 5:13-15 Is any among you afflicted? let him pray. Is any merry? let him sing psalms. Is any sick among you? let him call for the elders of the church; and let them pray over him, anointing him with oil in the name of the Lord: And the prayer of faith shall save the sick, and the Lord shall raise him up; and if he have committed sins, they shall be forgiven him.

What does getting healed have to do with having our sins forgiven? You cannot separate the forgiveness of sin and healing. It is all throughout the scriptures.

The gospel is healing every sickness and every disease among the people. Isn't it interesting that we find here that suffering and sickness are two completely different things? If they were the same, why would he say here "is anyone suffering?" And then "is anyone sick?" It says that if you are suffering, then you pray. But it says if you are sick, come and let the elders pray.

So go ahead and get rid of the theory that with your sickness, you are suffering for Christ. If you say that, then you are saying that it is God's will for you to be sick. If you do not know how to pray, then refer to Romans 8:26 where it says that the Spirit helps in our infirmities.

This word "infirmities", in the Greek, actually means "weakness".

The kind of weakness that we are talking about the kind of weakness that Paul speaks of in,

2 Corinthians 12:9 And he said unto me, My grace is sufficient for thee: for my strength is made perfect in weakness. Most gladly therefore will I rather glory in my infirmities, that the power of Christ may rest upon me.

He was actually saying, "Though I am weak, I am strong. I can do all things through Christ who strengthens me." He was talking about the power of God, which comes on us when our flesh gets out of the way.

HUMILITY'S GOT THE POWER

When we understand that God does not need us, but He wants us and allows us to be a part of what He is doing, then we are weak and in a humble state of mind. That is the state of weakness that Romans 8 means when it mentions "infirmities." When we boast in our weakness and know that we cannot do anything of ourselves that is when we will have power. We do not get power by boasting about all of the signs, wonders and miracles that we are moving in. It is when I come among you and determine that I know nothing except Christ and Him crucified. Yet Paul knew more than all of the Corinthians. He was a man who considered himself, among all of the other apostles, weak and as nothing. That is why he boasted when he was weak. He knew that when he could not get things done, that was when God was going to do things.

IT BEGINS AND ENDS IN HEALTH

Job 2:1-7 Again there was a day when the sons of God came to present themselves before the LORD, and Satan came also among them to present himself before the LORD. And the LORD said unto Satan, From whence comest thou? And Satan answered the LORD, and said, From going to and fro in the earth, and from walking up and down in it. And the LORD said unto Satan, Hast thou considered my servant Job, that *there is* none like him in the earth, a perfect and an upright man, one that feareth God, and escheweth evil? and still he holdeth fast his integrity, although thou movedst me against him, to destroy him without cause. And Satan answered the LORD, and said, Skin for skin, yea, all that a man hath will he give for his life.

But put forth thine hand now, and touch his bone and his flesh, and he will curse thee to thy face. And the LORD said unto Satan, Behold, he *is* in thine hand; but save his life. So went Satan forth from the presence of the LORD, and smote Job with sore boils from the sole of his foot unto his crown.

God was not the one who gave Job the sickness. People have many reasons they will argue of why Satan was permitted to strike Job with the boils, but the point is that God did not stretch forth His hand and give Job a sickness or disease. God healed him. Satan is the author of sickness and disease. That is why Jesus said, "I have come that you might have life, and life abundantly." The devil has come to kill, steal and destroy. Acts 10:38 How God anointed Jesus of Nazareth with the Holy Ghost and with power: who went about doing good, and healing all that were oppressed of the devil; for God was with him.

If He healed all of those who were oppressed of the devil, does that mean that every deaf ear, blind eye, epileptic, paralytic, fever driven person was oppressed of the devil? Absolutely!

To those who believe that some sickness if from God, why did Jesus heal ALL of the sick in this passage of scripture? This was a great multitude of people. Sickness, disease and death came into the earth through sin in the garden.

It all came in under the curse of the law. We have been redeemed from the curse of the law, but can choose to live in willful sin and rebellion and, by that, remove ourselves from under His umbrella of grace.

Isn't it interesting that God started the beginning of the Bible or the history of the earth, without sickness, disease and death and ends it the same way? Revelation 22 talks about a river, and leaves of the trees are for the healing of the nations. Yet, we are not seeing in North America the miracles and healings that we are going to see. If we will read everything that the word says about healing and begin to rid ourselves of the spirit of unbelief, and ask God to help our unbelief, then we will begin to see the greater works that we are called to do.

Miracle Road Blocks

You must check every road block so you can remove them all and receive your miracle. There are many road blocks, to healing in the church today. These are some of the reasons healing can be hindered in our lives and ministries. Please pray that God would speak to you if there is a hindrance to healing in your life. I simply offer a few reasons why miracles can be blocked. I pray this new Chapter will help you receive and effectively minister healing.

LITTLE FAITH Greek: Oligopistos, small, and pistis faith "describing a faith that lacks confidence or trusts too little. It is also referred to as "undeveloped faith" as opposed to outright unbelief.

Undeveloped faith is the faith that grows like a mustard seed when action is applied to knowledge.

Examples of this word are found in these verses:

Matthew 8:26 And he saith unto them, Why are ye fearful, O ye of little faith? Then he arose, and rebuked the winds and the sea; and there was a great calm.

Matthew 14:31 And immediately Jesus stretched forth *his* hand, and caught him, and said unto him, O thou of little faith, wherefore didst thou doubt?

Matthew 16:8 *Which* when Jesus perceived, he said unto them, O ye of little faith, why reason ye among yourselves, because ye have brought no bread?

They forgot to take bread and they feared they would starve.

This happened twice after they had an opportunity to develop and use faith. They saw God feed the 5,000 and the 4,000 with only a few loaves and fish. God expected more from them because of what they had already seen.

UNBELIEF

Mark 6:1 And he went out from thence, and came into his own country; and his disciples follow him.

Mark 6:5, 6 And he could there do no mighty work, save that he laid his hands upon a few sick folk, and healed *them*. And he marvelled because of their unbelief. And he went round about the villages, teaching.

There is more than one kind of unbelief, like personal unbelief that hinders healing. There is unbelief in a city like Nazareth that can hinder the corporate healing. Also there can be unbelief in a nation or generation can hinder healing as well.

Matthew 17:19, 20 Then came the disciples to Jesus apart, and said, Why could not we cast him out? And Jesus said unto them, Because of your unbelief: for verily I say unto you, If ye have faith as a grain of mustard seed, ye shall say unto this mountain, Remove hence to yonder place; and it shall remove; and nothing shall be impossible unto you.

UNFORGIVENESS In this passage of scripture (above), Jesus describes how one servant was forgiven a big debt and then that same servant failed to forgive his servant of a small debt. The man forgiven the bigger debt after begging his master for forgiveness did not show the same mercy he received to his servant, so the Lord turned him over to the tortures.

Matthew 18:34, 35 And his lord was wroth, and delivered him to the tormentors, till he should pay all that was due unto him. So likewise shall my heavenly Father do also unto you, if ye from your hearts forgive not every one his brother their trespasses.

There is a direct link to sickness and unforgiveness. The word for torture and torment here means: agony of body and mind, torment by demons inflicting intense pain to the body or mind. Scientific tests have concluded anger causes high blood pressure, heart problems and disease.

Bitterness also causes mental problems, cancers and chronic conditions.

Matthew 6:14, 15 For if ye forgive men their trespasses, your heavenly Father will also forgive you: But if ye forgive not men their trespasses, neither will your Father forgive your trespasses.

Matthew 5:23-25 Therefore if thou bring thy gift to the altar, and there rememberest that thy brother hath ought against thee; Leave there thy gift before the altar, and go thy way; first be reconciled to thy brother, and then come and offer thy gift. Agree with thine adversary quickly, whiles thou art in the way with him; lest at any time the adversary deliver thee to the judge, and the judge deliver thee to the officer, and thou be cast into prison.

This passage describes offenses and how God doesn't just want us to be sure we are not offended but that if we know one offended us we are to go to them and be peace makers. There are many times I had to make the choice to not to be offended again. Many of you are in a place where you know another has an issue with you and you are right.

I can not help it if they are offended, I did nothing. For the sake of your brother or sister, lay down your gift at the altar and go be reconciled. If you make the first step even though you have no offence, if they stay offended, at least you are free. God's healing came for Job by forgiving those who judged him and were even wrong. Many people say I am not asking forgiveness for something I did not do wrong.

Job 42:10-13 And the LORD turned the captivity of Job, when he prayed for his friends: also the LORD gave Job twice as much as he had before. Then came there unto him all his brethren, and all his sisters, and all they that had been of his acquaintance before, and did eat bread with him in his house: and they bemoaned him, and comforted him over all the evil that the LORD had brought upon him: every man also gave him a piece of money, and every one an earring of gold. So the LORD blessed the latter end of Job more than his beginning: for he had fourteen thousand sheep, and six thousand camels, and a thousand yoke of oxen, and a thousand she asses. He had also seven sons and three daughters.

INTIMACY God is asking us, will you have relationship with me? Will you pray and go deeper.

John 6:2 And a great multitude followed him, because they saw his miracles which he did on them that were diseased.

Jesus wanted them to know the bread of heaven. The people wanted God for what he did and the blessing. Jesus said I want heart relationship.

John 6:53, 54 Then Jesus said unto them, Verily, verily, I say unto you, Except ye eat the flesh of the Son of man, and drink his blood, ye have no life in you. Whoso eateth my flesh, and drinketh my blood, hath eternal life; and I will raise him up at the last day.

SIN

James 5:16 Confess *your* faults one to another, and pray one for another, that ye may be healed. The effectual fervent prayer of a righteous man availeth much.

Jesus spoke to the man crippled 38 years at the pool about sin and sickness.

John 5:14 Afterward Jesus findeth him in the temple, and said unto him, Behold, thou art made whole: sin no more, lest a worse thing come unto thee.

PRAYER AND FASTING When there is not enough prayer and fasting it can also hinder healing in our life.

Matthew 17:21 Howbeit this kind goeth not out but by prayer and fasting.

Psalms 35:13 But as for me, when they were sick, my clothing *was* sackcloth: I humbled my soul with fasting; and my prayer returned into mine own bosom. I behaved myself as though *he had been* my friend *or* brother: I bowed down heavily, as one that mourneth *for his* mother.

Isaiah 58:6 *Is* not this the fast that I have chosen? to loose the bands of wickedness, to undo the heavy burdens, and to let the oppressed go free, and that ye break every yoke?

Isaiah 58:8 Then shall thy light break forth as the morning, and thine health shall spring forth speedily: and thy righteousness shall go before thee; the glory of the LORD shall be thy rereward.

PRIDE

2 Kings 5:10, 11 And Elisha sent a messenger unto him, saying, Go and wash in Jordan seven times, and thy flesh shall come again to thee, and thou shalt be clean. But Naaman was wroth, and went away, and said,

Behold, I thought, He will surely come out to me, and stand, and call on the name of the LORD his God, and strike his hand over the place, and recover the leper.

Naaman nearly failed to receive healing because of his pride and position.

I have been in meetings where God would not heal somebody because they judged in a pride attitude. I don't have to go up to the front to be healed; or I am not falling down. They resist God through pride and fear of losing position if there seen having a man lesser or younger than them pray for them. Be first at the altar to receive from children and young people.

Respond to the man of God, I will do anything the Lord says. I don't care if I seem vulnerable and somebody might think why he is at the altar. Our ministry facade may hinder the blessing of healing because too many times we are the ones doing ministry to the people to receive from another is to suggest we do not have it together.

RELIGIOUS SPIRIT AND ATTITUDES

Matthew 11:16, 17 But whereunto shall I liken this generation? It is like unto children sitting in the markets, and calling unto their fellows, And saying, We have piped unto you, and ye have not danced; we have mourned unto you, and ye have not lamented.

In this passage, Jesus describes a generation that misses God because they want predictive Christianity. They want to orchestrate how the people respond and when. It is tradition and formulas that can hinder God's healing power. We want to keep in control. If we play the flute, the people dance.

Matthew 11:1 And it came to pass, when Jesus had made an end of commanding his twelve disciples, he departed thence to teach and to preach in their cities.

The religious spirit wants to challenge God even after miracles happen and are evident. They say I won't believe unless God does this kind of a healing, or if God heals the sick, prove it to us then and heal this one (Usually the one crippled.)

Keys to Receiving Your Miracle

Luke 11:54 Laying wait for him, and seeking to catch something out of his mouth, that they might accuse him.

A religious spirit wants to find the faults and criticize and judge. They are in a place where they can not receive from God because they are in, "I will find something wrong, I knew it attitude."

They have already made up there mind, watching for an error, rather than a touch me mindset and humbly saying "God if it's real please touch me."

2 Timothy 3:5 Having a form of godliness, but denying the power thereof: from such turn away.

And from such people turn away!" Religious forms can hinder the healing power of Jesus. When we are more concerned about keeping the tradition, time, rules, methods and appearances it hinders the manifest power of Jesus.

LIMIT GOD

Psalms 78:41 Yea, they turned back and tempted God, and limited the Holy One of Israel.

We limit God in many ways to a word of knowledge or a package. We fail to receive because it has to happen in this style or through this scenario. God can only heal when this is happening or God only heals some. We limit God in our expectation and shut God out of doing it any other way than unless this one or that one lays hands on me.

FEAR

Job 3:25 For the thing which I greatly feared is come upon me, and that which I was afraid of is come unto me.

Many times fear is the door the enemy uses to pass along generational sickness when we believe we are going to inherit this because my Mother and great, great Grandmother had it. Fear kept them out of the land of promise and the fear of a few spies spread too many. Saul was called out as king and to appear before the people but his fear kept him hiding in the baggage equipment. When we see the giants of opposition in our life, the doctor's reports or the impossible situation itself, it can inspire fear which can not only cause, but hinder healing in our lives.

UNSCRIPTURAL DOCTRINES

Matt 22:29 Jesus answered and said to them, You are mistaken, not knowing the Scriptures nor the power of God.

Do you know what a stronghold is? A stronghold is when we have believed a lie.

It is a thinking pattern and process of thoughts patterned after what we believe because of what we have heard or experienced.

I have met many that have failed to receive healing in their bodies because they have heard and been taught that God only heals some or think that miracles passed 2000 years ago. God uses sickness as Fathers discipline, Paul's thorn in the flesh. It is a part of suffering for Jesus. Even though they do not believe that those religious doctrines have been known to hinder healing today?

DEMONS

Demons not only cause but hinder healing today. Sometimes it is not a matter of praying for healing, but casting out devils.

Luke 13:10, 11 Now He was teaching in one of the synagogues on the Sabbath. And behold, there was a woman who had a spirit of infirmity eighteen years, and was bent over and could in no way raise herself up.

Matthew 17:14-15 And when they had come to the multitude, a man came to Him, kneeling down to Him and saying, Lord, have mercy on my son, for he is an epileptic and suffers severely; for he often falls into the fire and often into the water.

Isaiah 61:3 The garment of praise for the spirit of heaviness;

Mark 9:25 When Jesus saw that the people came running together, He rebuked the unclean spirit, saying to it, Deaf and dumb spirit, I command you, come out of him and enter him no more!

Matt 9:32-33 As they went out, behold, they brought to Him a man, mute and demon-possessed. And when the demon was cast out, the mute spoke and the multitudes marveled, saying, It was never seen like this in Israel!

Matthew 12:22 Then one was brought to Him who was demon possessed, blind and mute; and He healed him, so that the blind and mute man both spoke and saw.

Acts 10:38 how God anointed Jesus of Nazareth with the Holy Spirit and with power, who went about doing good and healing all who were oppressed by the devil, for God was with Him.

EXCUSES

John 5:7 The sick man answered Him, Sir, I have no man to put me into the pool when the water is stirred up; but while I am coming, another steps down before me.

Nobody laid hands on me. I am too sick to get to the meeting. They did not call out my word of knowledge. I am not worthy. They did not pray long enough for me. I can not make a commitment. I work all the time. I can't get in that line of a hundred so I won't get prayer. I have to leave by 9:00 pm. Excuses blame everyone and everything else for our not received healing.

MOTIVE

Matt 11: 7-9 As they departed, Jesus began to say to the multitudes concerning John: "What did you go out into the wilderness to see? A reed shaken by the wind? But what did you go out to see? A man clothed in soft garments? Indeed, those who wear soft clothing are in kings' houses. But what did you go out to see? A prophet? Yes, I say to you, and more than a prophet.

What did you go out to see? Did you go to receive a word or to be wowed? Is it the he man or does the package offend you. What are your expectations?

John 6:26 Jesus answered them and said, Most assuredly, I say to you, you seek Me, not because you saw the signs, but because you ate of the loaves and were filled.

You just want the blessing and benefit.

1 John 5:14-15 Now this is the confidence that we have in Him, that if we ask anything according to His will, He hears us. And if we

know that He hears us, whatever we ask, we know that we have the petitions that we have asked of Him.

These motives can be a hindrance to healing because many times we ask God amiss and we want to be healed, so we can go on eating the foods that cause illness. Will we change our lives, our eating and nutrition? Sometimes our motive is self glory. I told the John Lake story about a man who heard a crippled boy lost and crying out on the mountain.

This man made sure no one was looking and ran over and healed him before anyone could see it was him and then took of before anyone could attach his name to the miracle.

COMPLAINING, MURMURING & GRUMBLING

Numbers 21: 4-5 Then they journeyed from Mount Hor by the Way of the Red Sea, to go around the land of Edom; and the soul of the people became very discouraged on the way. And the people spoke against God and against Moses: Why have you brought us up out of Egypt to die in the wilderness? For there is no food and no water, and our soul loathes this worthless bread.

Negative Confessions

I knew it would happen to me, I always get sick. I deserve this because, I never receive from God. God why did you heal her they don't deserve it I do. God never blesses me. Why should I tithe it doesn't change anything. Why pray it's too hard? God doesn't speak to me anyway why the word read.

Murmuring, "why does this happen to me?" God, "why did you bring us here?" It was better over there.

Psalms 78:18-20 And they tested God in their heart by asking for the food of their fancy. Yes, they spoke against God: They said, Can God prepare a table in the wilderness? Behold, He struck the rock, So that the waters gushed out, and the streams overflowed. Can He give bread also? Can He provide meat for His people?

Psalms 78: 32, 33 In spite of this they still sinned, and did not believe in His wondrous works. Therefore their days He consumed in futility, and their years in fear.

DISOBEDIENCE Many times we can fail to receive healing because we will not do what the Lord say's. Whether it is to forgive, jump in the pool 7 times, do something you could not do. Many times we are disobedient to the Lord's strategies for our healing. Steps of obedience release healing. Has God spoken to you about an area of obedience? Have you responded?

John 2:5 His mother said to the servants, Whatever He says to you, do it.

Do whatever He tells you. I know people that refuse to respond to a word of knowledge or separate themselves from an area of sin. I have been in meetings where God ask people to do something in faith they could not do and they refuse because they say I don't feel or see change. What if God told us to spit in an eye or on a tongue? The blessing came to the widow's house in the days of Elijah because she was obedient to the Lords word.

1 Kings 17:11-16 And as she was going to get it, he called to her and said, Please bring me a morsel of bread in your hand. So she said, As the Lord your God lives, I do not have bread, only a handful of flour in a bin, and a little oil in a jar; and see, I am gathering a

couple of sticks that I may go in and prepare it for myself and my son, that we may eat it, and die. And Elijah said to her, Do not fear; go and do as you have said, but make me a small cake from it first, and bring it to me; and afterward make some for yourself and your son. For thus says the Lord God of Israel: The bin of flour shall not be used up, nor shall the jar of oil run dry, until the day the Lord sends rain on the earth. So she went away and did according to the word of Elijah; and she and he and her household ate for many days. The bin of flour was not used up, nor did the jar of oil run dry, according to the word of the Lord which He spoke by Elijah.

PRAYERLESSNESS

2 Kings 20:1-6 In those days Hezekiah was sick and near death. And Isaiah the prophet, the son of Amoz, went to him and said to him, Thus says the Lord: Set your house in order, for you shall die, and not live. Then he turned his face toward the wall, and prayed to the Lord, saying, Remember now, O Lord, I pray, how I have walked before You in truth and with a loyal heart, and have done what was good in Your sight. And Hezekiah wept bitterly. And it happened, before Isaiah had gone out into the middle court, that the word

of the Lord came to him, saying, Return and tell Hezekiah the leader of My people, Thus says the Lord, the God of David your father: I have heard your prayer, I have seen your tears; surely I will heal you. On the third day you shall go up to the house of the Lord. And I will add to your days fifteen years. I will deliver you and this city from the hand of the king of Assyria; and I will defend this city for My own sake, and for the sake of My servant David.

We need to be like the persistent widow. When the disciples ask Jesus how to pray effectively his response was do not give up until it happens.

Luke 11:5-8 And he said unto them, Which of you shall have a friend, and shall go unto him at midnight, and say unto him, Friend, lend me three loaves; For a friend of mine in his journey is come to me, and I have nothing to set before him? And he from within shall answer and say, Trouble me not: the door is now shut, and my children are with me in bed; I cannot rise and give thee. I say unto you, Though he will not rise and give him, because he is his friend, yet because of his importunity he will rise and give him as many as he needeth.

Luke 18:1-8 And he spake a parable unto them *to this end,* that men ought always to pray, and not to faint; Saying, There was in a city a judge, which feared not God, neither regarded man: And there was a widow in that city; and she came unto him, saying, Avenge me of mine adversary. And he would not for a while: but afterward he said within himself, Though I fear not God, nor regard man; Yet because this widow troubleth me, I will avenge her, lest by her continual coming she weary me. And the Lord said, Hear what the unjust judge saith. And shall not God avenge his own elect, which cry day and night unto him, though he bear long with them? I tell you that he will avenge them speedily. Nevertheless when the Son of man cometh, shall he find faith on the earth?

Many times we fail to receive healing because we give up after not seeing immediate results.

The bible says in Heb 11:6 God is a rewarder of those who diligently seek him.?

UNGODLY ATTITUDES TOWARDS LEADERS

Numbers 16:1-3 Now Korah, the son of Izhar, the son of Kohath, the son of Levi, and

Dathan and Abiram, the sons of Eliab, and On, the son of Peleth, sons of Reuben, took *men:* And they rose up before Moses, with certain of the children of Israel, two hundred and fifty princes of the assembly, famous in the congregation, men of renown: And they gathered themselves together against Moses and against Aaron, and said unto them, *Ye take* too much upon you, seeing all the congregation *are* holy, every one of them, and the LORD *is* among them: wherefore then lift ye up yourselves above the congregation of the LORD?

I have seen this in the church today. People speak out against leaders because they feel that they are just or more anointed then them. Running from church to church or not even going. The worst sin is complaining and speaking against the leader or pastor. It's the lone wolf, lone ranger spirit, the spirit of division and undermining.

Numbers 16:31-33 And it came to pass, as he had made an end of speaking all these words, that the ground clave asunder that *was* under them: And the earth opened her mouth, and swallowed them up, and their houses, and all the men that *appertained* unto Korah, and all *their* goods. They, and all that *appertained* to them, went down alive into the pit, and the earth closed upon them: and they perished from among the congregation.

Numbers 12:1, 2 And Miriam and Aaron spake against Moses because of the Ethiopian woman whom he had married: for he had married an Ethiopian woman. And they said, Hath the LORD indeed spoken only by Moses? hath he not spoken also by us? And the LORD heard *it*.

Numbers 12:9, 10 And the anger of the LORD was kindled against them; and he departed. And the cloud departed from off the tabernacle; and, behold, Miriam *became* leprous, *white* as snow: and Aaron looked upon Miriam, and, behold, *she was* leprous.

Sometimes we need to repent for speaking out and criticizing others especially leaders and even moves of God or manifestations.

Remember Michal and how she became barren because she judged and spoke out against David as he danced before the Lord.

IGNORANCE Many times we fail to receive healing because we do not know what God's will is.

Hosea 4:6 My people are destroyed for lack of knowledge: because thou hast rejected knowledge, I will also reject thee, that thou shalt be no priest to me: seeing thou hast forgotten the law of thy God, I will also forget thy children.

NATURAL MEANS Sometimes God gives us good wisdom about nutrient, eating and vitamins. Still God can use doctors and medicine.

2 Kings 20:7 And Isaiah said, Take a lump of figs. And they took and laid *it* on the boil, and he recovered.

Remember healing still comes from God even if medicine is used.

OUR CONFESSION

Proverbs 18:20, 21 A man's belly shall be satisfied with the fruit of his mouth; *and* with the increase of his lips shall he be filled. Death and life *are* in the power of the tongue: and they that love it shall eat the fruit thereof.

Proverbs 15:4 A wholesome tongue *is* a tree of life: but perverseness therein *is* a breach in the spirit.

Proverbs 12:14 A man shall be satisfied with good by the fruit of *his* mouth: and the recompence of a man's hands shall be rendered unto him.

Proverbs 12:18 There is that speaketh like the piercings of a sword: but the tongue of the wise *is* health.

BROKEN SPIRIT

Proverbs 17:22 A merry heart doeth good *like* a medicine: but a broken spirit drieth the bones.

Proverbs 18:14 The spirit of a man will sustain his infirmity; but a wounded spirit who can bear?

Sometimes hindrances to healing can be a trauma and wounds of the past. We don't always need physical but emotional healing.

ANXIETY, FEAR, WORRY Sometimes what is going in our hearts can hinder our healing and even be the cause of sickness.

Proverbs 14:30 A sound heart *is* the life of the flesh: but envy the rottenness of the bones.

Proverbs 14:23 In all labour there is profit: but the talk of the lips *tendeth* only to penury.

HARDENED HEART Hardened means: To form a callous or petrify, make hard, spiritual deafness or blindness. Those who repeatedly resist the word become insensitive and lose the power of understanding.

Matthew 8:16-18 When the even was come, they brought unto him many that were possessed with devils: and he cast out the spirits with *his* word, and healed all that were sick: That it might be fulfilled which was spoken by Esaias the prophet, saying, Himself took our infirmities, and bare *our* sicknesses. Now when Jesus saw great multitudes about him, he gave commandment to depart unto the other side.

Our healing can be hindered when we fail to remember his works in the past. It causes the heart to become dull.

Psalms 78:9 The children of Ephraim, *being* armed, *and* carrying bows, turned back in the day of battle.

This happened after they forgot his past works the heart also becomes hardened by the deceitfulness of sin or even areas of little compromise and inward toleration.

Hebrews 3:12, 13 Take heed, brethren, lest there be in any of you an evil heart of unbelief, in departing from the living God. But exhort one another daily, while it is called To day; lest any of you be hardened through the deceitfulness of sin.

Hebrews 5:14 But strong meat belongeth to them that are of full age, *even* those who by reason of use have their senses exercised to discern both good and evil.

The cares of the world also cause the heart to become dull (Parable of sower) Rebellion is also a key to the heart being dull. When we continually resist the word or do not meditate on the word.

Ezekiel 12:1, 2 The word of the LORD also came unto me, saying, Son of man, thou dwellest in the midst of a rebellious house, which have eyes to see, and see not; they have ears to hear, and hear not: for they *are* a rebellious house.

NEGATIVE INFLUENCES

Mark 5:35 While he yet spake, there came from the ruler of the synagogue's *house certain* which said, Thy daughter is dead: why troublest thou the Master any further?

Jairus nearly lost his daughter because the people and the circumstances said give up.

Do not feed your spirit with negative people and those who are trying to keep you from what God really wants you to have. There will always be those negative voices speaking it is not God's time. Did you see what the report said? The devil wants you to focus on the contrary winds and will even use family and friends to try to discourage us. See nothing happened or If God did not heal me then why would he heal you. Why do you need to press in for healing isn't salvation enough? Bear it and grin it the Lord is teaching you. The woman whose son died and was raised from the dead had those discouraging voices.

2 Kings 4:23 And he said, Wherefore wilt thou go to him to day? *it is* neither new moon, nor sabbath. And she said, *It shall be* well.

Luke 18:39 And they which went before rebuked him, that he should hold his peace:

but he cried so much the more, *Thou* Son of David, have mercy on me.

GREED

2 Kings 5:20-27 But Gehazi, the servant of Elisha the man of God, said, Behold, my master hath spared Naaman this Syrian, in not receiving at his hands that which he brought: but, *as* the LORD liveth, I will run after him, and take somewhat of him. So Gehazi followed after Naaman. And when Naaman saw *him* running after him, he lighted down from the chariot to meet him, and said, *Is* all well? And he said, All *is* well. My master hath sent me, saying, Behold, even now there be come to me from mount Ephraim two young men of the sons of the prophets: give them, I pray thee, a talent of silver, and two changes of garments. And Naaman said, Be content, take two talents. And he urged him, and bound two talents of silver in two bags, with two changes of garments, and laid *them* upon two of his servants; and they bare *them* before him. And when he came to the tower, he took *them* from their hand, and bestowed *them* in the house: and he let the men go, and they departed. But he went in, and stood before his master. And Elisha said unto him, Whence *comest thou,* Gehazi? And he said,

Thy servant went no whither. And he said unto him, Went not mine heart *with thee,* when the man turned again from his chariot to meet thee? *Is it* a time to receive money, and to receive garments, and oliveyards, and vineyards, and sheep, and oxen, and menservants, and maidservants? The leprosy therefore of Naaman shall cleave unto thee, and unto thy seed for ever. And he went out from his presence a leper *as white* as snow.

It was Greed in the case of Simon the sorcerer that hindered him receiving an impartation of healing power.

Acts 8:18-20 And when Simon saw that through laying on of the apostles' hands the Holy Ghost was given, he offered them money, Saying, Give me also this power, that on whomsoever I lay hands, he may receive the Holy Ghost. But Peter said unto him, Thy money perish with thee, because thou hast thought that the gift of God may be purchased with money.

CURSE Many times we do not receive healing because we first need to break the curse of infirmity. Generational curses can cause sickness and disease.

Many times the same curse upon another in our family is passed down.

Deuteronomy 28:46 And they shall be upon thee for a sign and for a wonder, and upon thy seed for ever.

NO EXPECTATION

Acts 3:5 And he gave heed unto them, expecting to receive something of them.

Many people fail to receive healing today because our attitude is not aggressive enough. We sit back and wait to see if anything happens. If God wants to heal me he can do it here in my seat. I will take what he gives me. I guess it is his will because I am not healed. What about the story in Acts 12 after they pray all night for Peter to be released from prison. When he is released by an angel and knocks at the door they do not believe it is him. Many people in the church can pray all night but do we expect the answer is coming.

Acts 12:14-16 And when she knew Peter's voice, she opened not the gate for gladness, but ran in, and told how Peter stood before the gate. And they said unto her, Thou art mad.

But she constantly affirmed that it was even so. Then said they, It is his angel. But Peter continued knocking: and when they had opened *the door,* and saw him, they were astonished.

Miracles Happen Today

There are many reasons why people are able to receive their miracles. Now let's look at the reasons why miracles do happen.

Matthew 14:14 And Jesus went forth, and saw a great multitude, and was moved with compassion toward them, and he healed their sick.

God's compassion means: sympathy, pity, tender mercies and feeling of affection. The compassionate heart of God is the number one reason why miracles happen. Everything in the kingdom works through love, Faith worketh by love. In the beginning when God made a covenant with man through Abraham. It was the love of God that initiated the covenant of blessing.

God spoke to Abram and now Abraham.

Genesis 17:6-10 And I will make thee exceeding fruitful, and I will make nations of thee, and kings shall come out of thee. And I will establish my covenant between me and thee and thy seed after thee in their generations for an everlasting covenant, to be a God unto thee, and to thy seed after thee. And I will give unto thee, and to thy seed after thee, the land wherein thou art a stranger, all the land of Canaan, for an everlasting possession; and I will be their God. And God said unto Abraham, Thou shalt keep my covenant therefore, thou, and thy seed after thee in their generations. This *is* my covenant, which ye shall keep, between me and you and thy seed after thee; Every man child among you shall be circumcised.

What is a Covenant?

A covenant means, compact, contract, pledge, agreement. This can occur between individuals, kings and his people, God and his people, or marriage.

God's covenant with Abraham is the eternal foundation stone of Israel's relationship with God and all other bible promises are based on this one. God wanted man to receive all his blessing, goodness and benefits of salvation so when he cut covenant with Abraham he passed through the first offering initiated through love the first blood sacrifice.

Genesis 15:17 And it came to pass, that, when the sun went down, and it was dark, behold a smoking furnace, and a burning lamp that passed between those pieces.

Hebrews 6:13 For when God made promise to Abraham, because he could swear by no greater, he sware by himself,

Remember with any other covenant when one party fails to hold up to his end of the bargain legally we are released from the binding contract. God knew that if he didn't take it upon himself to initiate and fulfill the covenant man would break it in our sin nature. God so loved the world he gave of Himself! God is still giving to us whom are in covenant with Him.

GOD IS BOUND TO HIS WORD Titus 1:2 In hope of eternal life, which God, that cannot lie, promised before the world began;

1 Peter 2:24 Who his own self bare our sins in his own body on the tree, that we, being dead to sins, should live unto

righteousness: by whose stripes ye were healed.

GOD WILLS IT The willingness of Jesus is he wants to. We don't have to jump through all the healing hoops and beg.

Matthew 8:2, 3 And, behold, there came a leper and worshipped him, saying, Lord, if thou wilt, thou canst make me clean. And Jesus put forth *his* hand, and touched him, saying, I will; be thou clean. And immediately his leprosy was cleansed.

Matthew 8:6, 7 And saying, Lord, my servant lieth at home sick of the palsy, grievously tormented. And Jesus saith unto him, I will come and heal him.

MASS EVANGELISM The number one tool for soul winning is the miraculous. John 6:2 And a great multitude followed him, because they saw his miracles which he did on them that were diseased.

Matthew 4:24, 25 And his fame went throughout all Syria: and they brought unto him all sick people that were taken with divers diseases and torments, and those which were possessed with devils, and those which were lunatick, and those that had the palsy; and he healed them. And there followed him great multitudes of people from Galilee, and *from* Decapolis, and *from* Jerusalem, and *from* Judaea, and *from* beyond Jordan.

Acts 4:15, 16 But when they had commanded them to go aside out of the council, they conferred among themselves, Saying, What shall we do to these men? for that indeed a notable miracle hath been done by them *is* manifest to all them that dwell in Jerusalem; and we cannot deny *it*.

DEMONSTRATION OF DEITY When Jesus heals the cripple man lowered from the roof by his friends.

Mark 2:5-7 When Jesus saw their faith, he said unto the sick of the palsy, Son, thy sins be forgiven thee. But there were certain of the scribes sitting there, and reasoning in their hearts, Why doth this *man* thus speak blasphemies? who can forgive sins but God only?

Mark 2:10, 11 But that ye may know that the Son of man hath power on earth to forgive sins, (he saith to the sick of the palsy,) I say unto thee, Arise, and take up thy bed, and go thy way into thine house.

When Jesus did this miracle, the statement to the scribes was if you believe in the God of your father David, you believe that only God can forgive sin and heal. Jesus knew that the scribes believed the promise in,

Psalms 103:2 Bless the LORD, O my soul, and forget not all his benefits:

When the miracle happened they would have to believe he could forgive sin because only God can heal and forgive, thus making him God. He turned water into wine to demonstrate his deity.

John 2:11 This beginning of miracles did Jesus in Cana of Galilee, and manifested forth his glory; and his disciples believed on him.

The works he did, demonstrates he is God.

John 14:11 Believe me that I *am* in the Father, and the Father in me: or else believe me for the very works' sake.

FULFILL THE PROPHETIC WORD Isaiah 53:5 But he *was* wounded for our transgressions, *he was* bruised for our iniquities: the chastisement of our peace *was* upon him; and with his stripes we are healed.

Matthew 8:16, 17 When the even was come, they brought unto him many that were possessed with devils: and he cast out the spirits with *his* word, and healed all that were sick: That it might be fulfilled which was spoken by Esaias the prophet, saying, Himself took our infirmities, and bare *our* sicknesses.

FAITH James 5:15 And the prayer of faith shall save the sick, and the Lord shall raise him up; and if he have committed sins, they shall be forgiven him.

Mark 11:24 Therefore I say unto you, What things soever ye desire, when ye pray, believe that ye receive *them,* and ye shall have *them.*

Matthew 9:22 But Jesus turned him about, and when he saw her, he said, Daughter, be of good comfort; thy faith hath made thee whole. And the woman was made whole from that hour.

Matthew 9:27-29 And when Jesus departed thence, two blind men followed him, crying, and saying, *Thou* Son of David, have mercy on us. And when he was come into the house, the blind men came to him: and Jesus saith unto them, Believe ye that I am able to do this? They said unto him, Yea, Lord. Then touched he their eyes, saying, According to your faith be it unto you.

Matthew 8:13 And Jesus said unto the centurion, Go thy way; and as thou hast believed, *so* be it done unto thee. And his servant was healed in the selfsame hour.

John 4:50 Jesus saith unto him, Go thy way; thy son liveth. And the man believed the word that Jesus had spoken unto him, and he went his way.

Luke 17:19 And he said unto him, Arise, go thy way: thy faith hath made thee whole.

HEALING ANOINTING Habakkuk 3:4, 5 And *his* brightness was as the light; he had horns *coming* out of his hand: and there *was* the hiding of his power. Before him went the pestilence, and burning coals went forth at his feet.

The presence of Jesus drives sickness away.

Luke 5:17 And it came to pass on a certain day, as he was teaching, that there were Pharisees and doctors of the law sitting by, which were come out of every town of Galilee, and Judaea, and Jerusalem: and the power of the Lord was *present* to heal them.

Luke 6:19 And the whole multitude sought to touch him: for there went virtue out of him, and healed *them* all.

PROVE THE MINISTRY Acts 2:22 Ye men of Israel, hear these words; Jesus of Nazareth, a man approved of God among you by miracles and wonders and signs, which God did by him in the midst of you, as ye yourselves also know:

1 Kings 17:24 And the woman said to Elijah, Now by this I know that thou *art* a man of God, *and* that the word of the LORD in thy mouth *is* truth.

HE IS RISEN Jesus is alive and continues to prove the resurrection.

Hebrews 13:8 Jesus Christ the same yesterday, and to day, and for ever.

Revelations 1:18 *I am* he that liveth, and was dead; and, behold, I am alive for evermore, Amen; and have the keys of hell and of death.

Jesus demonstrates the resurrection through healing and delivering people from death, sickness and disease.

HEALING COMMISSION John 14:12 Verily, verily, I say unto you, He that believeth on me, the works that I do shall he do also; and greater *works* than these shall he do; because I go unto my Father.

Mark 16:15-18 And he said unto them, Go ye into all the world, and preach the gospel to every creature. He that believeth and is baptized shall be saved; but he that believeth not shall be damned. And these signs shall follow them that believe; In my name shall they cast out devils; they shall speak with new tongues; They shall take up serpents; and if they drink any deadly thing, it shall not hurt them; they shall lay hands on the sick, and they shall recover.

Matthew 10:1 And when he had called unto *him* his twelve disciples, he gave them power *against* unclean spirits, to cast them out, and to heal all manner of sickness and all manner of disease.

Matthew 10:7, 8 And as ye go, preach, saying, The kingdom of heaven is at hand. Heal the sick, cleanse the lepers, raise the dead, cast out devils: freely ye have received, freely give.

REPENTANCE With every miracle comes, a responsibility to change and healings can be a judgment against whole cities. Matthew 11:21-23 Woe unto thee, Chorazin! woe unto thee, Bethsaida! for if the mighty works, which were done in you, had been done in Tyre and Sidon, they would have repented long ago in sackcloth and ashes. But I say unto you, It shall be more tolerable for Tyre and Sidon at the day of judgment, than for you. And thou, Capernaum, which art exalted unto heaven, shalt be brought down to hell: for if the mighty works, which have been done in thee, had been done in Sodom, it would have remained until this day.

God expects a change in our lives when he touches us. Psalms 78:12 Marvellous things did he in the sight of their fathers, in the land of Egypt, *in* the field of Zoan.

God divides the Red sea, leads them with a pillar of cloud by day and fire at night, gives them drink from the rock, manna from heaven, quail meat to eat, deliverance from Egypt and all these miraculous signs and still; they sinned.

Psalms 78:17 And they sinned yet more against him by provoking the most High in the wilderness.

TO BELIEVE IN THE SUPERNATURAL God does signs and wonders today so we will believe in his power to do the impossible. For example we have the story of Lazarus.

John 11:3-5 Therefore his sisters sent unto him, saying, Lord, behold, he whom thou lovest is sick. When Jesus heard *that,* he said, This sickness is not unto death, but for the glory of God, that the Son of God might be glorified thereby. Now Jesus loved Martha, and her sister, and Lazarus.

God waits two days and seems to be late and Lazarus dies. The Lords response is: John 11:15 And I am glad for your sakes that I was not there, to the intent ye may believe; nevertheless let us go unto him.

He said I am glad, why? That YOU MIGHT BELIEVE!

John 20:30, 31 And many other signs truly did Jesus in the presence of his disciples, which are not written in this book: But these are written, that ye might believe that Jesus is the Christ, the Son of God; and that believing ye might have life through his name.

GOODNESS Matthew 7:11 If ye then, being evil, know how to give good gifts unto your children, how much more shall your Father which is in heaven give good things to them that ask him?

GOD IS SOVEREIGN Ecclesiastes 8:3 Be not hasty to go out of his sight: stand not in an evil thing; for he doeth whatsoever pleaseth him.

When God was filling people mouths with Gold crowns and teeth in our meetings and people asked why, I struggled with why do we always have to ask why? I knew it was God. Lives were being healed, saved and changed. God spoke to me and said I do what I want to.

I do believe that God has a purpose in what he does but I am ok with not always understanding why he does it one way and he seems to contradict what I know or expect. God knows how to do things out of the box.

THE GOSPEL Miracles happen because of the good news.

Romans 1:16 For I am not ashamed of the gospel of Christ: for it is the power of God unto salvation to every one that believeth; to the Jew first, and also to the Greek.

Romans 16:19 For your obedience is come abroad unto all *men.* I am glad therefore on your behalf: but yet I would have you wise unto that which is good, and simple concerning evil.

Paul the Apostle just made an amazing statement. He suggested that if we are not preaching the gospel in Mighty signs and wonders, we are not preaching the full gospel.

FRIENDSHIP WITH GOD John 15:15, 16 Henceforth I call you not servants; for the servant knoweth not what his lord doeth: but I have called you friends; for all things that I have heard of my Father I have made known unto you. Ye have not chosen me, but I have chosen you, and ordained you, that ye should go and bring forth fruit, and *that* your fruit should remain: that whatsoever ye shall ask of the Father in my name, he may give it you.

God hears the prayers of His friends. Whatever you ask the Father in my name He will give you.

THE GLORY OF GOD Matthew 15:31 Insomuch that the multitude wondered, when they saw the dumb to speak, the maimed to be whole, the lame to walk, and the blind to see: and they glorified the God of Israel.

John 9:3 Jesus answered, Neither hath this man sinned, nor his parents: but that the works of God should be made manifest in him.

God does miracles in situations where He, and not man, will be glorified.

I remember a story about a man who heard a crippled boy lost and crying out on the mountain. This man made sure no one was looking, and ran over and healed him before anyone could see it was him, and then left before anyone could attach his name to the miracle.

CURSE OF THE LAW Galatians 3:13, 14 Christ hath redeemed us from the curse of the law, being made a curse for us: for it is written, Cursed *is* every one that hangeth on a tree: That the blessing of Abraham might come on the Gentiles through Jesus Christ; that we might receive the promise of the Spirit through faith.

God wants us to receive the blessing of Abraham. To be free from the curse is to be released of all diseases.

Desperation Mark 5:27 When she had heard of Jesus, came in the press behind, and touched his garment.

To push her way through the crowd and risk the consequences of the law, being unclean with an issue of blood and arrested. This woman should be kept outside the camp. Mark 10:46-48 And they came to Jericho: and as he went out of Jericho with his disciples and a great number of people, blind Bartimaeus, the son of Timaeus, sat by the highway side begging. And when he heard that it was Jesus of Nazareth, he began to cry out, and say, Jesus, *thou* Son of David, have mercy on me. And many charged him that he should hold his peace: but he cried the more a great deal, *Thou* Son of David, have mercy on me.

He cried out all the more. We must press in beyond the fear of what others think and cry out. Matthew 15:22-28 And, behold, a woman of Canaan came out of the same coasts, and cried unto him, saying, Have mercy on me, O Lord, *thou* Son of David; my daughter is grievously vexed with a devil. But he answered her not a word. And his disciples came and besought him, saying, Send her away; for she crieth after us. But he answered and said, I am not sent but unto the lost sheep of the house of Israel. Then came she and worshipped him, saying, Lord, help me. But he answered and said, It is not meet to take the children's bread, and to cast *it* to dogs. And she said, Truth, Lord: yet the dogs eat of the crumbs which fall from their masters' table. Then Jesus answered and said unto her, O woman, great *is* thy faith: be it unto thee even as thou wilt. And her daughter was made whole from that very hour. It is time to let nothing get in the way of our healing.

TO DESTROY THE DEVILS WORK Acts 10:38 How God anointed Jesus of Nazareth with the Holy Ghost and with power: who went about doing good, and healing all that were oppressed of the devil; for God was with him.

How many did He heal and whom?

Jesus only healed those oppressed of the devil. But He healed every sickness and disease among the people. Could it be in God's eyes all sickness and disease is a work of the devil? 1 John 3:8 He that committeth sin is of the devil; for the devil sinneth from the beginning. For this purpose the Son of God was manifested, that he might destroy the works of the devil.

NAME OF GOD

Exodus 15:26 And said, If thou wilt diligently hearken to the voice of the LORD thy God, and wilt do that which is right in his sight, and wilt give ear to his commandments, and keep all his statutes, I will put none of these diseases upon thee, which I have brought upon the Egyptians: for I *am* the LORD that healeth thee.

When God assigns a name in the bible, that name carries with it the person's nature and destiny. God name is Jehovah Rapha in this verse!

Rapha: To cure, heal, repair, mend, and restore health, one who heals; is the Hebrew word for doctor. The main idea of Rapha is physical healing. Healing is the character of God and He can never be anything other than who He is. I am the Lord and I change not.

COMMUNION 1 Corinthians 11:29, 30 For he that eateth and drinketh unworthily, eateth and drinketh damnation to himself, not discerning the Lord's body. For this cause many *are* weak and sickly among you, and many sleep.

If you can be sick and die prematurely for not taking from the Lords' table properly, you can also be healed through communion by taken it correctly.

GIFTS OF THE SPIRIT 1 Corinthians 12:9, 10 To another faith by the same Spirit; to another the gifts of healing by the same Spirit; To another the working of miracles; to another prophecy; to another discerning of spirits; to another *divers* kinds of tongues; to another the interpretation of tongues:

THE NAME OF JESUS God heals the lame man at the gate of beautiful and is the answer to why the name of Jesus is why miracles happen.

Acts 3:6 Then Peter said, Silver and gold have I none; but such as I have give I thee: In the name of Jesus Christ of Nazareth rise up and walk.

Acts 3:16 And his name through faith in his name hath made this man strong, whom ye see and know: yea, the faith which is by him hath given him this perfect soundness in the presence of you all.

FILLED WITH THE SPIRIT The nature of the Holy Spirit is creation and makes healing happen. Where the Holy Spirit is moving, creation happens.

Genesis 1:2 And the earth was without form, and void; and darkness *was* upon the face of the deep. And the Spirit of God moved upon the face of the waters.

Romans 8:11 But if the Spirit of him that raised up Jesus from the dead dwell in you, he that raised up Christ from the dead shall also quicken your mortal bodies by his Spirit that dwelleth in you.

The presence of the Holy Spirit anointed Jesus with power to do healing, and we are now temples of the Holy Spirit. The healing anointing doesn't come from above but from within. You are carrying it now.

SALVATION

Do we know that we are saved? What is salvation?

Luke 7:50 And he said to the woman, Thy faith hath saved thee; go in peace.

Saved in this passage is the Greek word Sozo: To save, heal, cure, preserve, keep safe and sound, rescue from danger or destruction, deliver. Sozo saves from physical death through healing and spiritual death by forgiveness of sin and its effect. Simply put on a new heart and a new life. We find this Greek word in this passage for healing.

Mark 6:56 And whithersoever he entered, into villages, or cities, or country, they laid the sick in the streets, and besought him that they might touch if it were but the border of his garment: and as many as touched him were made whole.

Romans 10:9 That if thou shalt confess with thy mouth the Lord Jesus, and shalt believe in thine heart that God hath raised him from the dead, thou shalt be saved.

Kingdom The last reason for why I can expect to be healed and see miracles is the kingdom.

Matthew 6:10 Thy kingdom come. Thy will be done in earth, as *it is* in heaven.

Jesus made the statement here that is not just on earth now as it is in heaven but I want it to be on the earth now as it is in heaven. How is it in heaven now? There is no sorrow, pain, sickness, poverty, disease, death, sin and more. God's kingdom brings the realities of heaven on earth.

Matthew 12:28 But if I cast out devils by the Spirit of God, then the kingdom of God is come unto you.

God I ask on behalf of the person reading this that You will cover them with your love right now.

Keys to Receiving Your Miracle

God take them down which ever path they need to go down to receive their miracle. I command everything in their body that is not of God to disappear in Jesus mighty name, Amen.

About The Author

Bill Vincent is no stranger to understanding the power of God. Not only has he spent over twenty years as a Minister with a strong prophetic anointing, he is now also an Apostle and Author with Revival Waves of Glory Ministries in Litchfield, IL. Along with his wife, Tabitha, he, leads a team providing apostolic oversight in all aspects of ministry, including service, personal ministry and Godly character.

Bill offers a wide range of writings and teachings from deliverance, to experiencing presence of God and developing Apostolic cutting edge Church structure. Drawing on the power of the Holy Spirit through years of experience in Revival, Spiritual Sensitivity, and deliverance ministry, Bill now focuses mainly on pursuing the Presence of God and breaking the power of the devil off of people's lives.

His books 48 and counting has since helped many people to overcome the spirits and curses of Satan. For more information or to keep up with Bill's latest releases, please visit www.revivalwavesofgloryministries.com. To contact Bill, feel free to follow him on twitter @revivalwaves.

Keys to Receiving Your Miracle

Recommended Books

By Bill Vincent

Overcoming Obstacles
Glory: Pursuing God's Presence
Defeating the Demonic Realm
Increasing Your Prophetic Gift
Increase Your Anointing
Keys to Receiving Your Miracle
The Supernatural Realm
Waves of Revival
Increase of Revelation and Restoration
The Resurrection Power of God
Discerning Your Call of God
Apostolic Breakthrough
Glory: Increasing God's Presence
Love is Waiting – Don't Let Love Pass You By
The Healing Power of God
Glory: Expanding God's Presence
Receiving Personal Prophecy
Signs and Wonders
Signs and Wonders Revelations
Children Stories
The Rapture
The Secret Place of God's Power
Building a Prototype Church
Breakthrough of Spiritual Strongholds

Keys to Receiving Your Miracle

Glory: Revival Presence of God
Overcoming the Power of Lust
Glory: Kingdom Presence of God
Transitioning to the Prototype Church
The Stronghold of Jezebel
Healing After Divorce
A Closer Relationship With God
Cover Up and Save Yourself
Desperate for God's Presence
The War for Spiritual Battles
Spiritual Leadership
Global Warning
Millions of Churches
Destroying the Jezebel Spirit
Awakening of Miracles
Deception and Consequences Revealed
Are You a Follower of Christ
Don't Let the Enemy Steal from You!
A Godly Shaking
The Unsearchable Riches of Christ
Heaven's Court System
Satan's Open Doors
Armed for Battle
The Wrestler
Spiritual Warfare: Complete Collection
Growing In the Prophetic
Faith
The Angry Fighter's Story
Understanding Heaven's Court System

Web Site:
www.revivalwavesofgloryministries.com

Keys to Receiving Your Miracle

www.ingramcontent.com/pod-product-compliance
Lightning Source LLC
Chambersburg PA
CBHW052102070526
44584CB00017B/2295